XCIX

d.p. houston

2021

by the same ███████

---

*England's Green
Hairball Surprise!*

*Project Sonnet
The World According to the Confessions of Lasser Vice*

"How dare there be poets?"

ishmael smith

This is a **Grating Wringer Press** publication.

ISBN: 978-1-326-07885-0

99 Rexxxxd Sonnets by *d.p. houston*

© 2021

First printed in 2019; a few copies, for private distribution.
This edition, with corrections & adjustments, 2021.

list of contents

heretic's menu

Should reason fail, you'll still have what it takes :
Analysis is often no great shakes.

cohort of ammunition

My original (we'd better say *initial*) plan was for a broad collaboration of 14 different ▮▮▮, each contributing 14 ▮▮▮▮▮ to accumulate a total of 196 redacted ▮▮▮▮▮▮/▮▮▮▮▮▮ sonnets. I emailed a proposal (14 points, natch) with the proviso that it be sent on to anyone who might be interested. Only one set of 14 came back; after six months, it was still the only offering*. In the meantime, I'd come up with quite a few more of my own and it seemed best to abandon the collaborative 196 plan, and go for a selfish 99 instead. Whether the other six named contributors are my ▮▮▮, or I'm one of theirs, is moot.

Some of the ▮▮▮▮▮ are taken from ▮▮▮▮ that have been ▮▮▮▮▮▮ previously. Some conclude *possible* ▮▮▮▮ that may, eventually, be ▮▮▮▮; others are likely to remain foundlings, sustained by fantasies of loving, interesting, brutal, high-born, low-life, or cruelly mistreated missing ▮▮▮ bodies.

The idea evolved when I was dipping into a recently published anthology of work from the ▮▮▮▮ ▮▮▮▮▮. This might explain the brief, infrequent outbreaks of ▮▮▮ that attentive readers will probably notice. Once I'd resolved to finish it myself, the project also came to feel like comment on (and embodiment of) the condition of being ▮▮▮▮; it appears that on the whole ▮▮▮ are no longer ▮▮▮▮'s unacknowledged ▮▮▮▮▮. Unacknowledged *period*, more like, if you don't mind. Boo bloody hoo. In any case, this ▮▮▮ thread was not one I could reasonably ignore, having produced a look-at-me-but-fuck-off object last ▮▮▮ in the form of my sealed ▮▮▮▮▮▮▮.

Perhaps the appetite (for gobbets) stimulated by the fluttering attention-spans of social media was another factor. Most of these ▮▮▮▮ would fit in a greetings-card or, for those prepared to squint a bit, on a scrap of paper in a for-▮▮▮ cookie. If commercial cinema is any guide, a decent pay-off may be all you really need. (▮▮▮ and cinema: try ▮▮▮ ▮▮▮, by ▮▮▮ ▮▮▮, a story included in ▮▮▮ ▮▮, 1998.)

As for the darkened ▮▮▮ themselves, I have tried (in the spirit of the ▮▮▮ ▮▮▮'s *creative constraint*) to arrange them on the page in a manner that suggests the ▮▮▮▮▮▮ as well as the rungs of a cage.

*chapeau – and apologies – to ▮▮▮▮▮▮

7

d.p. houston

i :   *the ref Donne reveres*

Nobody cares what the drowning man drinks **:**
everyone cheers when that idiot sinks.

ii :   *rhymester's gyration*

Fear's ever-present, like knots without string :
what's changed, exactly? Hell, hardly a thing.

iii :   *limits unfold*

Say what you like about freedom of speech :
some of this shit makes the mind scream for bleach.

iv : *a stagnant air hit*

Fruitless the fiddler who scratches and gawps **:**
maggots must thrive in Love's beautiful corpse.

v :   *pen universal*

Some can't be cured by a trip to the vet :
sex with a stranger is Russian roulette.

vi :   ***unarmored betimes***

Shadowy torches keep passion in thrall :
light without darkness is nothing at all.

vii : *in beaux, his charm*

Orgulous lion or innocent pup :
good Lord above will still fuck your ass up.

viii :   ***retraced ellipsis***

L'esprit d'escalier's lips got there first :
."bonniest *mots* are the ones you've rehearsed."

ix : *double ten, a growing whelp*

So evening ends with the draught that calms :
a cold pint of milk in The Nurse's Arms.

x : ***butt, artisan anoints***

As from thy piss the sweetest lemonade,
so from these farts a fine fanfaronade.

xi : ***merciless, must sure***

At this *la Belle*'s exquisite nostrils flared **:**
"c'est qui, ce con anglais, bordel de merde?"

xii :   *legibly, so soon*

A dream through which Ma Nature drives a truck :
how in the hell do doctors ever fuck?

xiii :   *ego, shine there not*

With luck the mystery will take a chair,
love sometimes being neither here nor there.

xiv : *ears mourn deep seas*

And then you'll know precisely what he meant :
the bench is level and the garden's bent.

tender Atlas tilts

Georgina Micross

i : *rankest legend's whittling hews*

None lead, none leave : let mystery adorn
this ring of footprints on our frosted lawn.

ii : *torn mess*

Seek out the dusk. Hang doubt in high esteem.
Grant those who lie to sleep an honest dream.

iii :   *an uncool hat*

One long term lasts - *anacoluthon*'s hired,
and Trump picks up his cards; snap, all are fired.

iv :   *nerves' oneness*

Conversion's the thing - with fixed grins we sing
for Impiety's holiest blessing.

v :   *idolaters, we*

a grateful prisoner and eager prey.
(I'll struggle if you like. What do you say?)

vi : ***fig - my oeuvre - eve***

*(From fever, in truth, I desire no release;
this knot, no untying; this passion, no peace.)*

vii :   ***chopper's feast***

The space between words is where honesty purrs.
The sound of your eyes is where passion's bull stirs.

viii : **do but to bud**

Like quite a lot that seeks to please the ears,
it's not as charming as it first appears.

ix : *hung foe's fun*

Captivated targets grin and leer
pretending to be insincere.

x : *tidy scripture*

(Analysis suggests the missing pair
is lost on purpose, and was never there.)

xi : ***absurd toxic ruse***

Futile the flowers that garland your halls :
Time keeps a castle with blood on the walls.

xii :   *Nacho piggy*

(Grant us release from this mendacious Puck -
sewers rebranded are still full of muck.)

xiii : **_cut out all cruel_**

this holy echo-chamber, cold and vast,
where angry children mass to scold the past.

xiv :   ***tether space***

What rot. The changeling hoards can hog the dark.
I'll still be carrying a torch for Petrarch.

desonnet

i : when twilight's gentle darkness
ii : monsters
iii : anacoluthon
iv : nonsense verse
v : least wired O
vi : you give me fever
vii : parts of speech
viii : doubt...doubt
ix : Enough Snuff
x : Dirty Pictures
xi : obscuritas redux
xii : hypagognic
xiii : call-out culture
xiv : teacher's pet

Eliza Stonefils

i :   *"Mr Emotion, me"*

Best body of work for this well-read class **:**
a mawkish carcass with a feisty arse.

ii :   *à* **Sonia Agonos**

long past your last chance to get shit to work,
up to your eyes in malevolent murk.

iii : *Mr Noun's verisimilitude*

How hideous the horrors of acclaim :
how intimate the microscopes of shame.

iv :   *said Smith*

enquire if Lady Muck takes bribes in cash
and pray to Christ shebangs like this don't crash.

v :   *Godly Manoeuvres*

lust's hopeful ghost stuck like ashes in coal,
and your heart an insatiable sinkhole.

vi :   *top pros beg*

and watch the tireless wagging of that chin
in binding perpetuity begin.

vii :   *für* **Avril Gunseit**

They want to know if I've been saved - like what?
A falling baby or a goal-bound shot?

viii : *cheeky longevity rebooted*

It all depends if Meaning's *horloge* chimes :
no pun on *pun* when John Donne *spunne*, betimes?

ix : *por* **Maxime MaCapaul**

your sorry excuse for mitigation
gives little thanks to prayer inflation.

x :   *heritage of Grief*

Come, Sir, tuck in - follow Death - be a binger :
sought-after monuments glisten like Ginger.

xi : *row now holy dildos*

tinder to fuel a contrarian crowd,
zero fucks given and all heads unbowed.

xii : **secret arias reveal alien's true love**

"Buttbreak and Horsecock, report to Cell 6.
New fish wants schooling **:** break time into ticks."

xiii :   ***twig a finite bone***

because all that thou couldst, that thou hast done -
nothing remains for remonstrance to shun.

xiv : *semantic ass recitals*

your idiot bliss and bad poetry,
made for each other like dogpiss and tree.

Routine's Fettle

i : memento mori
ii : anosognosia
iii : de Mortuis nil nisi verum
iv : shit Midas
v : love's young dream
vi : gobstopper
vii : virtue signal
viii : yoked by violence together
ix : mea maxima culpa
x : a fig for thee, Geri
xi : Hollywood Windsor
xii : la tracasserie nouvelle est arrivée
xiii : agenbite of inwit
xiv : a critical assessment

Sonia Agonos

i : **_hue blocker_**

Contagious anhedonia will get
you in the end. (*Yeah? Wanna fucking bet?*)

ii : *__pray Nirvana's hype__*

honeymoon's motto **:** *adieu, rêves de cul.*
(Married reality's arselessly dull.)

iii :   ***trump hot namesake***

perhaps the best advice he's ever had :
you stand up straight, the bitch-tits ain't so bad.

iv : *arguing back, five meek*

now you're resolved, like some sadistic perve,
to make a trophy of my last live nerve.

v : *capable, urgent, erect*

Would it be laying it on rather thick
if I was sorry to have been that prick?

vi :   *starlets quit lightly*

Hey, *enfant terrible*, *épate* that *nourrice!*
Finish the function with grease in her crease.

vii : *these impersonal thighs alienate song*

See how he wields that incontinent hose,
shooting so hard it drips out of her nose.

viii :   *toad's off*

a dirty gift dispensed by Lady Luck **:**
the pleasure of a good, hot, cheap McFuck.

ix :   *livid vet tell alien tale*

Light the way dimly that leads us to bed :
near-sighted lovers give much the best head.

x :   *salty layover*

Spread your wings wide so he'll know who to thank
next time he pulls a spectacular wank.

xi : *union-oiling epigrams*

But swagger such as his should raise a flag :
he'll fuck you like he's stubbing out a fag.

xii :   *spoilt non-U*

Froideur will curse my ardour as uncool,
parce que la vie (comme d'habitude) s'encule.

xiii :   *inset orchids*

The mind's eye prickles when you come so close.
If I could shoot you up I'd overdose.

xiv :   *impotent serenade*

now that man is an autoentomber.
(Just shut the fuck up, fool - OK, Boomer?)

Cocky gun cut fountain?

i : blue choker
ii : happy anniversary
iii : posture maketh man
iv : give me a fucking break
v : unacceptable regret
vi : ghastly little squirt
vii : the harlots's pen is something else again
viii : fast food
ix : live and let live a little
x : loyalty saver
xi : reimagining Polonius
xii : toi non plus
xiii : shit I'd censor
xiv : endtimes on repeat

Avril Gunseit

i : **best oiled**

du liebst mich dieser Tage nicht zu sehr -
vielleicht kommt etwas Böses auch daher.

ii :   *caged fauna taunt*

Spurn as you must the sad song this clown sings :
serious people do sensible things.

iii : *anteater's porpoise porno*

and when you're far enough away, look plumb :
you'll see me tiny, trapped, a spider's crumb.

iv :   *blood unwed*

The time has surely come to pay the price
for every time you had to ask me twice.

v : **_star shags a ghoul_**

We strive to see through this inverted night,
bedazzled by the darkness of Delight.

vi : *vim's exegetic foes*

recalling quantitative data's bluff :
ample sufficiency's never enough.

vii :   *crappy dice admit*

The road, though empty, is a well-worn track :
the rules, while thorough, carry much-loved slack.

viii : *unseeing my quest*

bent by the powers that be in her bonnet,
busy as any Shakespearean sonnet.

ix :   *intransitive exams*

Questions like this will make misery glad :
what if I'm better than merely not bad?

x :   *see, vulgar ruffians*

the fool frustrated in his master-plan
to be considered an important man.

xi :   *ease not stoats*

for now is the time, silly goose, to turn
in digital fire where nothing can burn.

xii : *parse equal anomaly*

This final opening makes hay with pawns :
Death's ghastly overture draws in its horns.

xiii :   *academic osculation*

this lonesome iteration of regret
will see you mourned by friends you've never met.

xiv :   *i.e. nether hole*

and (however much this must seem odd) bless.
Nuff said? There, a headstone for the godless.

hi, Rev Zen!

i : Liebestod
ii : cantata and fugue
iii : a proportionate response
iv : double down
v : as through a glass
vi : give me excess of it
vii : didactic mappery
viii : stingy Queen Muse
ix : vanitas in extremis
x : universal suffrage
xi : season to taste
xii : play on a square meal
xiii : social media account
xiv : here lieth one

Maxime MaCapaul

i : *morn's harmless clot*

It's always like this when you go to war,
flickering matches at a man of straw.

ii :   *mad Joy simmers*

So stand with dream-clean eyes to find your bliss,
and give that butterfly a Glasgow Kiss.

iii : *gnawing sooth*

An explanation has proved hard to get :
Lord Know-Almighty remains in our debt.

iv : ***usual grim audit***

One tongue-blessed time before the lights are dimmed,
you'll know the ardent bliss of being hymned.

v : *heat fed faint of heart*

because it's no fun when your *cinq à sept*
is only there because they lost a bet.

vi : ***abattoir moon***

Don't tell a soul why your lies wear a hood :
incontinent honesty's no bloody good.

vii : *sunset's dependence*

Send me to jail in a golf-club blazer,
and shave my balls with a cut-throat razor.

viii :   *hex mental keel*

Whinnying naysayers balk as you please **:**
I hear my father whenever I sneeze.

ix :   *doubt at sham Zen*

How the gods relish our preposterous
focus on remaining pre-posthumous.

x : *angular sentience*

May your marmoreal *pensées* be bound
while foes rot in unconsecrated ground.

xi : ***rewriting zippy neon***

bland, formless, endlessly fucking polite
apotheosis of the purest shite.

xii : ***not namesake, this***

Forgive me but it's true - some sins lie best
if they remain forever unconfessed.

xiii :   *to forgo only*

and pack your precious blessings in a hearse :
awareness of awareness is a curse.

xiv :   *warning-shot exam*

the chances of a song called *Jeu d'Esprit*,
composed by Chic, performed by Judas Priest.

Come, comic panto mice!

Tony Logo

i :   *elegy loot*

Reasoning backwards is good for a laugh -
post-hoc pro-bono : who's whose better half?

ii :   *poet's oily gem*

Meaning of meaning's an infinite tease :
brainiac blowhards look good on their knees.

iii :   *churning realities*

like some poor fool busted for smuggling dope,
tethering air at the end of a rope.

iv :   *lycra's eye-claw*

Never mind which way your tendencies bend -
most of us end up as food in the end.

v : *bushy, barefaced end*

Listen up closely as Fate yanks your chain :
what you can hear is us feeling no pain.

vi :   ***top slag potty - lol***

Nothing you try will be right - *quoi qu'on fasse,*
Brits speaking French are just *trop dégueulasses.*

vii : *unbleached on-trend*

The wise leave worldly vengeance on the shelf :
once in a while a shit will flush itself.

viii : *arty charlatan poop*

Ponder and fear what the Jack of Cups said :
"Sober my arse - I'll dry out when I'm dead."

ix :   *ink's viable dress*

Telling twists a serpent from a stick
and rolls into the horrorshow's last flick.

x :   *legible elder ummers*

What's that thing called that you can't quite recall?
(Wossname aphasia comes for us all.)

xi : *E.T. in cataclysmic hope*

Track-marks of this dolly's parting shot
in eyeless orbit of a childlorn cot.

xii : ***Dido's Soul inches ahead***

and contemplate what's really in Loch Ness :
I'll show you smarmy fuckers *mindfulness*.

xiii :   *toke my germ*

stable-lads' line when they're stuck in a queue :
Hurry it up, mate - we got shit to do.

xiv :   *lychee net*

Freedom from form is a meaningless feat :
count on the patter of metrical feet.

list poet's halftone

i : teleology
ii : epistemology
iii : heuristic learning
iv : always recycle
v : Schadenfreude, baby
vi : polyglottal stop
vii : clean round the bend
viii : an apocryphal tarot
ix : darkness visible
x : glue remembered ills
xi : metaphysical conceit
xii : doc Shiels in da-da house
xiii : Greek Tommy
xiv : entelechy

Index of ████████

anderswo

Boîte de Vers (inner lid)
California Quarterly
Literary Review
poeticdiversity.org
thepotomacjournal.com
Project Sonnet
the World according to the Confessions of Lasser Vice

(too much information)

titles translated
endnotes
fourteen titles
can't you fucking count?
vierzehn
comme ça, on compte ici!
the set of all points